I'M NOT SELFISH, I'M SELF FIRST

I'M SELF FIRST

And It's Non-negotiable!

Mark Parris

I'm Not Selfish, I'm Self First,
And It's Non-negotiable
© 2023 by Mark Anthony Parris

For information contact

Cine Enigma Productions,

3702 W Spruce St #1006, Tampa, FL 33607

813-599-8396

Published by Cine Enigma Productions

Identifiers:
Library of Congress Control Number:
2023917101
ISBN 9798988692102 (paperback)

ISBN 9798988692126 (paperback)

ISBN 9798988692119 (e-book)

www.imselffirst.com

Acknowledgment

I would like to express my heartfelt gratitude to my mother, Jean Parris, and my father, Thomas Alan Parris, for their unwavering support and love throughout my life. I am also grateful for the love and joy brought into my life by my sons, Marc-Andrew, and Anthony, and my daughter, Ryan.

I appreciate my brothers Rawle, Bryan, Kevin and Nigel, my sisters Melanie and Colleen, my cousins Miles, Mark, Smiley, Brian, Michelle, Mollie, uncle Ken, auntie Jean and the rest of my family. Your presence and support have been invaluable to me.

To my close friends Gary Curry, Ray Balgrove, Tony Stinyard, Benjy Myaz, Errol Lyons, Nickai, Askell, Garfield, Mr. Bailey, Joe Restaino, Kevin, Rich, Cristian, Rockmond Dunbar, Mark Lewis, Abdel Campbell, Paul Campbell, Oso, Joe Matias, Sam Yeboah, Earl Bernard, Oneil, Granville, Wes, Mr. Pusey, and Desi and Don King, I am grateful for your friendship and positive impact on my life.

A special thank you goes out to the 34th Street crew, John Small, Rob Blaise, and Mario Fontus, as well as my day ones, Cheick Dukuly and Coolie Ranx. Your loyalty and friendship have been a source of strength for me.

I would also like to express my gratitude to the amazing women in my life who have been a source of inspiration, including Neyi, Tashana, Tiffani, Corine, Shelly, Kathy, LaToya, Trina, Wasana, Sherine, Rugina Castillo, Adama, Jaime, Ms. Blaise, Ira Rose, Ali, Ms. Hamilton, Donna, Shawna Lee, Ashantie, Cookie, Marsha, Monti, Dianne, Ruschiene, Jeanne, Shavon, Samantha,

Caasi, Camille, Minnie, Daphne Grant, Sheron, Julie, Evelyn George, Mrs. Bailey, Jenese Morris, Lory, Mrs. Pusey, Arti, Mrs. A, Maxine, Ameca, Sharon, and Shanice.

I would be remiss if I didn't acknowledge the influence and inspiration I have gained from LaTiesha Rivera in the creation of this book. Her impact on my creative journey has been invaluable.

Lastly, I would like to honor and remember my grandmother, Elmina Parris, my grandfather, Harper Parris, my Aunt Enid, Bryan Ivey, and my uncle, Sigmund Winter. Though they are no longer with us, their love and guidance continue to inspire me.

I am immensely grateful to everyone who has touched my life in one way or another. Your presence has contributed to my spiritual journey in ways that words cannot fully express. Thank you.

Contents

"There is a big difference between being
Self First and Being Selfish"

Prologue

I learned the hard way that constantly putting others and their needs before my own, can have negative consequences. In a world where some people take advantage of those who give too much, it's crucial to set boundaries. Prioritize your own needs. This doesn't mean disregarding others. It means you have a better understanding of Self.

By taking care of your Self first, you can tap into your true potential and unlock the power of manifestation. You are put in a better position of clarity; you can observe what is happening around you, and how you can respond. Of course, this requires understanding your inner Self.

That's where this book comes in. It's a guide to help you embark on a journey of self-discovery and unlock your transformational abilities.

Always remember, your inner God resides within, and connecting with it is essential.

CHAPTER 1

DISCOVERING
YOURSELF

Discovering your true self is a journey that sometimes takes a lifetime! For so long, we were so sure. We think we know ourselves pretty well. But then the need to discover who we truly are sneaks up, and we find ourselves with endless questions along the way and a melting pot of confusion. *"How did I get here?"* It's usually a test that comes along and shifts not only our belief system but also our belief in who we are as a person. It's when we begin to look at ourselves from a skewed perspective.

This test that I'm referencing, can come in so many versions. It can be a test of your moral fiber, a test of how much tolerance you possess, a test of your mental fortitude or a test of how well you know yourself.

The truth is, it's rare for people to be completely honest when evaluating themselves. We often showcase an idealized version of ourselves that we hope will be more likable or desirable. Because we sometimes have this need to be validated, we are clothed in emotional and mental disguise with the hope that we consistently receive the seal of approval. However, when put to the test, our true selves are revealed.

Moral Fiber

Let's examine the first test - the test of moral fiber. We are supposed to tell right from wrong. Because the lines between right and wrong can be blurred however, many people might argue that this is subjective; many will say it cannot be viewed in black and white. It will depend on the situation.

From this perspective, intentions are then looked at very closely to uncover the motive of our actions, and then we look at the effects of those actions to see whether they were done out of love. Were these intentions pure in nature? It is the realization of this close scrutiny that reveals the truth: Sometimes we must lose our way to find our way.

"Sometimes we must lose our way to find our way"

So, let's address the blurred lines that we struggle with when choosing right from wrong. One clear indication is when we get a feeling in our gut when something just doesn't feel right. You know what I am talking about. At some point in our lives, we have all experienced this. Many of us listen to that feeling.

Unfortunately, many of us ignore it, only to later regret that decision. I encourage you to start looking at your gut as your internal GPS. Trust your gut! The answers might not be immediate, but it's there to guide you in the right direction.

Here is something that we all forget. Life begins in the gut! When you are in the triple darkness of your mother's womb, it is the umbilical cord that sustains you and gives you the necessary vitals until birth.

At childbirth, the stem cells are passed from the mother to the child via that same umbilical cord to the gut. These stem cells are the building blocks of life and play a crucial role in our health and well-being. They help to repair damaged tissues, boost our immune system, and promote overall healing.

From the very beginning, gut health is imperative in order to survive. When we understand this, we make our lives that much easier. See your gut as the epicenter for all things that we know. Everything that you will ever need for the rest of your life has been downloaded from generation to generation through this very same process.

We have a tendency to look outward for the answers, while all the answers lay deep within us. We just need to pay attention, tap into that innate spiritual bank and manifest our truth. It's through this spiritual journey, we discover ourselves and who we really are.

But what does that spiritual journey look and feel like? Let me say this first of all, this spiritual journey is personal. It involves connecting with something greater than us and we access it in different ways. Many of us only think about a spiritual journey and the need to find our true Self when faced with some type of adversity.

But this is not the only way to set forth on a spiritual journey. There is also the time when we get sick and tired of being sick and tired. When we get to this point in time, we yearn and are moved to seek better. We make a conscious decision to be better. We become deliberate in our quest to access the truth that is deep within.

What I am talking about is not ephemeral. And because of this, it's the kind of journey that requires courage, patience and an unwavering commitment to self-discovery. It's about facing our fears head-on, embracing vulnerability and learning to let go of the things that no longer serve us. This is not easy work. In fact, it is a lifetime of active and proactive learning! But not only is it doable, it is necessary if we want to live a life filled with purpose and meaning.

What you need to always remember is, you are not alone. That which is greater than yourself - whether you call it God, the Universe or simply higher consciousness - will guide you towards your true path in life.

When we understand this Everlasting Presence as the center of our being and open ourselves up to this immutable connection, we can tap into a source of wisdom and guidance beyond what we could ever achieve on our own.

Even now, you might wonder, is it worth it? To embark on this journey is not easy. But what awaits you; knowing that everything changes for the better, is worth every challenging step you will take. We become more compassionate towards others as well as ourselves; more forgiving of mistakes made along the way; less judgmental of those who don't see things exactly as we do; happier overall because now every moment has meaning.

The spiritual journey isn't just some abstract concept reserved for monks living in remote temples, it's available right here and now for anyone willing to take that first step to claim what is your right to own.

Tolerance

Now let's move on to the test of tolerance. How much tolerance do you possess? How much can you put up with before you reach your boiling point? We all face this from time to time and more often than not, it is only when we are tested that we can evaluate just how far we can be pushed. Understanding this will help us discover our Self.

Of course, there are levels to this test. It could range from an outburst to causing bodily harm to someone. In other words, your tolerance level could climb from 1 to 10 in just seconds. And because this is possible, it is important that we know exactly what our boiling point is. It is important that we stand guard and not be triggered by fluctuating emotions.

Learn to see emotions for what they are: Thoughts that we give energy to. Without energy, they become fleeing thoughts. When we learn to control our minds and be in the know; when we practice mindful living, we defuse any chance of letting our emotions get the best of us.

We deflate the power of the ego and allow the existence of things that we do not necessarily like or agree with to occur without interference. Learn to release the need to control a situation; to be directed by your emotions and embrace the true power of being unbothered.

Keep in mind that people sometimes do things to get a reaction from us because it empowers them. The mere fact that someone can have that type of dominion over another person is quite bothersome and alarming. But we must keep in mind also that our response is under our control.

Think of it this way, we can react (knee jerk reflex) or respond (requiring thought) to a situation. In the medical world, it's a negative thing to 'having a reaction' to a medication, in contrast to 'responding to' that medication or treatment, which is a positive factor. We should govern ourselves in the same manner and respond rather than react to people or things. Take the extra time to think it through.

And once we understand our tolerance levels, how we choose to respond to a situation or person becomes a key component in the journey to discovering one's Self. Now we are empowered. Now we are on track to focus on the bigger picture.

In life, there will always be some form of distraction to unhinge us from our goals and aspirations. Accept this fact. See it as an integral part of life's journey. That is why it is crucial that we remain in the KNOW and the NOW.

Being in the know and in the now are key phrases that will shift your mind and add a positive trajectory to your life. You've heard it said before that, "When you know better you do better." Being 'in the know' is as simple as that.

We become better in that awareness. We strive to know and be the best version of ourselves. We understand the authenticity of our very existence. To do otherwise is to be counterproductive. To do otherwise is to ensure a mediocre way of life.

Mental Fortitude

When we are faced with adversity, the test of mental fortitude is on display. This is where preparing and strengthening our minds is a valid skill set that will help us to master any challenges we are faced with. Let's put this another way. It's about staying ready, so you don't have to get ready! This is what being 'in the now' is all about.

When we are faced with adversity, it's easy to feel overwhelmed and unsure of how to proceed. However, if we have prepared and strengthened our minds, we are better equipped to handle any challenges that come our way. The big question is, how do we go about preparing and strengthening our minds?

Honing this skill set includes cultivating a positive mindset, practicing resilience, and developing effective coping mechanisms. By doing so, we can approach difficult situations with a sense of calm and clarity, rather than succumbing to stress and anxiety.

It is important, however, to remember that this preparation is an ongoing process - we must continue to work on our mental fortitude in order to maintain our ability to master challenges. It's constant practice and reframing your mind until a renewed way of living becomes habitual.

Ultimately, being in the now means staying present and focused on the task at hand, rather than getting bogged down by worries about the future or regrets about the past. By staying ready, we can face adversity with confidence and strength.

"It's about staying ready so you don't have to get ready"

Know Yourself

Discovering our true self is an ongoing journey without a final exam. We are constantly evolving and striving to improve ourselves so we must keep this in mind. It's natural for our identity to change as we age - who we were at 18, 21, 30, and 35 are all distinct versions of ourselves. Failure to evolve would indicate a lack of growth or stagnation in life. Therefore, it's important to rediscover ourselves along the way and embrace the person we are becoming.

The different stages of change in Self might not be easy to accept and appreciate initially, simply because you are holding on to a selected image that you feel represents who you are. But when you freely embrace the different stages of becoming, your entire outlook is transformed. When you stay aware of this process and make a conscious effort to know yourself, no one will have the power of knowing you better.

Yes, it is a process that requires patience. But when you take the time to truly discover or rediscover who you are, it is an investment you will never regret. Cherish the moments of solitude to reflect on yourself. Don't hesitate to step out of your safe zone and try something new.

Try taking personality tests and assessments, and quiz yourself on your knowledge of Self. Discover how others view you; not because you are trying to bend to their will, but because you are on a mission to expand the vision of your Self. See it as your own personal audit.

Develop a 'Know Myself' questionnaire and tackle it with an open mind. So, talk with people. It could be a current partner or a previous one. It could be friends or a family member. Learn what they find intriguing and unique in addition to the things about you that annoy them.

Not all the answers will please you and that's ok. Just remind yourself that their feedback will provide a better understanding of how others perceive you. Now you have the information to compare with your own self-image. Now you can gain a better perspective and take the next step towards enlightenment.

These are the first steps needed to uncover the pathway to the discovery of Self. It's an awakening that needs to take place. Don't forget that we are all unique, so it really doesn't matter how you get to this point.

The important thing is that you arrive here. There is a world of opportunity waiting for you on the other side, filled with a life of purpose and passion that will leave you fulfilled every day. However, to reach this life, you must participate. You must take action.

It is time to stop settling for mediocrity and start striving for greatness. You have immense potential within you that is waiting to be unleashed. It all begins with making a decision today. Do not let fear or self-doubt hold you back any longer. You are capable of achieving anything your heart desires if you believe in yourself enough to try.

Therefore, I encourage you to choose greatness over complacency, and make the decision now that will change your life forever. Although the journey may not always be easy, rest assured that it will undoubtedly be worth it!

CHAPTER 2

UNDERSTADING YOUR PURPOSE OF SELF

Everything that we need to deal with what life throws our way, is buried deep within every single one of us. It is up to each and every person to dig deep within their souls to find what their purpose is on this journey that we call life. Through the exploratory method, we owe it to ourselves to live on the path of knowledge and understanding. To know yourself is to love your Self.

You recall that moment when the purpose of a gadget was suddenly revealed and it completely made your life that much easier? Well, the same can be said when one finds the true purpose of Self. That discovery…that clarity is the compass that makes life so much easier.

When we understand our true purpose, life becomes a journey of self-discovery and fulfillment. We are now able to tap into our inner resources and achieve greatness. With this power, we no longer feel lost or aimless. Instead, we have a clear direction and a sense of purpose that drives us forward.

This sense of purpose brings with it a deep sense of satisfaction and joy that permeates every aspect of our lives. We become more resilient in the face of challenges, more compassionate toward others, and more grateful for the blessings in our lives.

What is your purpose? If you're feeling lost or unsure about your path in life, it is time to reflect on your true purpose. You may be surprised at what you discover! In fact, you will question how life was before you came to that enlightenment. It's all within you.

We are born with everything that we will need in our lives, and that includes a purpose. Our unique Self is here for a reason and needs to be manifested. So, it is our job to uncover these answers throughout life's journey.

It's not enough, however, to simply know our purpose; we must also understand it. This is the error a lot of us make. We assume that one equates the other and we couldn't be more wrong.

Knowing about something doesn't always mean we understand it. For example, I may know about various processes, but not comprehend their underlying reasons. Therefore, we must actively take steps to progress from mere knowledge to true understanding. We have to be intentional and purposeful in all aspects of our lives.

Remember, "When you know better, you do better." When you understand your purpose of Self, you will not be easily unhinged. You will not be set off course. There will be distractions, but they will no longer have the capacity to derail you from your purpose or goals.

"When you know better, you do better."

Laser-like focus with your eyes and mind on the prize will be the way to live. You will be self-motivated while exuding an air of confidence. These are byproducts of understanding your purpose of Self. You see these traits in most of the successful people in today's world. They know and understand their purpose of Self and they will not sabotage or self-negotiate their position.

Being self-motivated and confident are crucial traits for success in any field. When you have a clear understanding of who you are and what you want to achieve, it becomes easier to stay motivated and confident in your abilities. Individuals who have achieved success today have devoted themselves to comprehending their purpose, enabling them to steer clear of self-sabotaging actions and jeopardizing their principles.

When you begin the journey of understanding Self and the dynamics of that revelation, it is necessary to remind yourself periodically that you have not embarked on an easy journey but a worthwhile one.

So, throughout these pages, there will be quick reminders just to keep us in check. And here is another one. Understanding your purpose of Self is not a one-time event; it's an ongoing process that requires constant reflection and evaluation. But it is worth it, every day!

Aligning ourselves with things that promote heightened consciousness are crucial aspects of understanding our purpose. Surrounding ourselves with people and things that help us progress toward enlightenment are essential. Just as a plant needs the right soil to flourish, and children require proper education to become successful adults, we need to seek out the right influences to align ourselves on the path toward self-realization.

Delve into your inner thoughts and explore the depths of your subconscious. Unleash the hidden treasures that lie within and discover your true purpose. Awaken the inner strength and power that reside within you. What do you need for this to happen? Time.

Take a conscious interest in who you are and set aside time to get to know you. This is crucial for your personal growth and success. Don't hesitate to push past any barriers that may be holding you back. You have the potential to achieve greatness so start now and unlock your full potential.

Understanding one's purpose has many layers. Some may only scratch the surface, while others proudly wear it as a badge of honor. Regardless of when it is discovered, it is important to make the most of it. Every aspect of life should be lived with intention and purpose. So, make it count!

It is crucial to comprehend the significance of your purpose in order to synchronize your actions with your objectives, leading to a more satisfying life, both personally and professionally. Devote ample time to delve into your purpose and experience a significant transformation in your trajectory.

CHAPTER 3

ENJOY YOUR SELF

Once you have taken the time to truly discover and understand your Self, it's important to allow yourself the opportunity to enjoy your own company. This is where you need to keep in mind that being alone does not mean you will automatically be lonely. It is what most people fear... being lonely. The truth is, when you spend time with yourself, you might find you are the best company ever! So, feel free to invest time and energy into activities that bring you joy and fulfillment. The activities will vary: it could be reading a book, watching a movie, going for a walk in nature or simply taking a relaxing bath. It doesn't matter what the activity is, as long as it makes you content; as long as you are focusing on taking care of number 1 – YOU!

This is what self-care is about. And here is another quick reminder; Self-care is not selfish. Self-care is an essential part of maintaining your overall welfare. By taking the time to enjoy yourself, you'll be better equipped to handle life's challenges with a clear mind and positive attitude. Just as others enjoy spending time with you because they appreciate your company, take some time to enjoy yourself as well.

Additionally, when you're able to appreciate your own company, you'll find that the relationships you forge with others will be that much stronger. That's because you can only truly know and understand those around you, when you know and understand yourself. Only then will you know where you fit in and what works.

So go ahead and indulge in some self-care today – you

deserve it! Embrace your true Self, not the persona you portray on social Media or the version of yourself that you wish to be. Remember, there is no substitute for being your authentic Self.

"Remember, there is no substitute for being your authentic Self."

It's important to recognize the value of enjoying your own company. If you don't find spending time with yourself enjoyable, why would someone else? Do you feel uncomfortable being alone? Don't give into that fear. Understand that you are enough and you deserve all that is good, and you don't have to depend on external company to fulfill your dreams.

Let me say this, nothing is wrong with wanting to have someone around. But when the need becomes so great that you can only function effectively with external forces, that's when you need to step back and recognize that you have lost a big chunk of who you are.

This makes it almost impossible for you to enjoy your own company. Make the change now. Start by identifying solo activities that bring you joy. Pursue them as often as you can. Take baby steps if necessary and understand why you have the need for constant companionship.

If you have the tendency to be clingy, explore why that is. Question your codependent behavior and work towards strengthening your belief in Self. The change will not happen overnight. But when you consistently invest the time to get to know more about you, in order to enjoy who you are, your transformation will be evident.

Think about all the benefits of spending time by yourself - you can do whatever you want without worrying about anyone else's preferences or opinions. You have complete control over how you spend your time and what activities you engage in. Not only that but spending quality solo time allows for introspection and self-reflection, which can lead to personal growth and development.

As I mentioned earlier, learning to enjoy your own company will improve your relationship with yourself, but also those in your inner circle as well. People are drawn toward individuals who exude confidence in their independence. So, take some steps today towards embracing solitude.

You have so many options available to you! You could try out a new hobby or simply take a walk alone. Remember, it doesn't matter what you choose. This is your investment in both present happiness as well as future relationships!

A lot of individuals put in a great deal of effort in their professional life and postpone their enjoyment until their retirement or some point in the future. However, when that time eventually arrives, will you be able to actually enjoy it?

Getting to know your Self and living in the present moment and being aware of what's happening can impact positively on the necessary steps to ensure that you can enjoy yourself. Begin enjoying yourself right now, at this very moment. Take pride in the fact that you possess all of your faculties and have been given a blank slate to create a wonderful picture of what your day holds.

Live your life to the fullest, starting right now, instead of waiting for tomorrow. You deserve to savor every moment and relish all the joys that life has to offer. Imagine waking up every morning with a sense of purpose, excitement, and achievement, knowing that you are making the most of your time here on earth.

Living in the now means taking charge of your current circumstances and building a future filled with happiness, success, and abundance. It entails setting achievable goals for yourself and working toward them one step at a time.

Don't let fear, doubt, or procrastination hold you back from living your best life. You have the power to create the reality that you desire and deserve. Start by identifying what truly brings you joy and fulfillment in life - whether it's pursuing a new career path, Traveling to exotic destinations or simply spending more quality time with loved ones.

Once you've identified your passions and goals, take action toward making them a reality. Don't wait for opportunities to come knocking on your door - go out there and seize them! Whether it means taking risks or stepping outside of your safe space, remember that every step forward is a step closer to achieving greatness.

And when obstacles inevitably arise along the way, don't give up! Use these challenges as opportunities for growth and learning. Remember that setbacks are not failures; they're merely temporary roadblocks on the journey toward success.

Wake up today and every day - and live boldly, dream big, and make every moment count. Your future self will thank you for it!

Having peace of mind requires being knowledgeable about all aspects of your life - such as finances and healthcare options - so that you can make wise decisions that will benefit you in the long run. By making informed choices, you can live your life to the fullest, free from anxiety and stress, and fully enjoy every moment that comes your way.

Don't wait another moment to start enjoying your life. Start with something small, yet meaningful today, like booking those plane tickets or signing up for that art class you've always wanted to try.

Always remember, life is too brief to not revel in every moment!

CHAPTER 4

AT PEACE WITH YOUR SELF

How do you acquire peace with Self? It is a state of mind that can be achieved through various practices. One way to achieve inner peace is through meditation, which helps to calm the mind and reduces stress. Another way is to practice gratitude, by focusing on the positive aspects of your life and being thankful for them. Whichever practice you choose – and you could choose to engage in the various attributes of many - it's also important to take care of your physical health by eating well, exercising regularly, and getting enough sleep. As you develop inner peace, the word to remember at all times, is balance.

Try not to overextend in any one area. Finding inner peace will require us to slow down our minds, quiet our thoughts, and bring stillness to our inner selves. It's important to let go of negative thoughts and emotions that will only drag us down. Negativity does not serve our purpose. Meditation is an excellent way to achieve these results. And I must add, there are different forms of meditation.

Find the one that works best for you. But generally, by taking deep breaths and releasing harmful and stagnant energies, we can connect to our inner selves and move beyond our minds and bodies. Breathing connects us from spirit to matter and back to spirit again, helping us achieve a sense of inner peace.

Purging daily negative thoughts and ideas can also aid in this goal. This is where we have daily mental 'house cleaning'. We cannot allow negative residues to get comfortable in our minds. Flush them out with our renewed breath and encourage only positivity to take root.

Another plus on this journey to inner peace is to surround ourselves with positive people who support and encourage you, as you reciprocate. Reciprocity is part of our balance and will contribute to a sense of inner peace. Additionally, it's helpful to set realistic goals and work toward achieving them at a pace that feels comfortable for you. Do not compare yourself with others. Each of us has a unique story and will approach the path in our own unique way.

We have to keep reminding ourselves that this is not a race, and the first at the finish line will receive a prize. Once you take the time to invest in your growth and by practicing these habits consistently, you can cultivate a sense of inner peace that will help you navigate life's challenges with greater ease and resilience.

I want to put the spotlight on gratitude for a minute. It's easy to overlook the importance of practicing gratitude in our lives. With the fast-paced nature of the world we live in, we often forget to stop and appreciate the blessings we have. And sometimes that means, just being able to take a breath.

We should remind ourselves that not everyone has the privilege of waking up each day. There are also individuals with disabilities who make the most out of their opportunities despite their limitations. It's crucial to shift our focus from what we lack and be grateful for what we possess and the circumstances we're in. We should also remember that there are people who would trade places with us, even if we think our situation is dire.

In Life, we can choose to walk in Love or walk in Fear. These powerful forces in the world are constantly at play, shaping our experiences and influencing our thoughts and actions. Love and fear represent the polarities that we must navigate in order to find balance and harmony in our lives. By being aware of these forces, we can learn to harness the power of love and overcome the grip of fear and find peace within us.

"In Life, we can choose to walk in Love or walk in Fear."

Fear is a powerful emotion that can hold us back from achieving our full potential and living the life we truly desire. It can prevent us from taking risks, pursuing our passions, and building meaningful relationships.

On the other hand, Love empowers us to live courageously and authentically. When we choose Love over Fear, we open ourselves up to new opportunities for growth and fulfillment.

So, I urge you today to make a conscious decision to walk in Love instead of Fear. Choose kindness over judgment, compassion over criticism, and forgiveness over resentment.

By doing so, you will not only improve your own well-being but also inspire others around you to do the same. Let's be willing ambassadors and spread love wherever we go because it has the power to change lives - including ours!

Remember, being in the KNOW means staying informed about what is happening around us and within us, while being in the NOW means living fully in the present moment. These two ingredients are essential for molding and shaping our minds, to survive in a world that often puts more credence in external validation over internal fulfillment.

Ensuring that you take good care of yourself is crucial for a life of sustenance and one that brings you peace. As previously mentioned, it all begins with your gut. Neglecting your gut health can have grave consequences. Consumption of processed foods, alcohol, and antibiotics can disrupt the delicate balance of bacteria in your gut microbiome, causing various health issues such as depression and autoimmune diseases like rheumatoid arthritis.

It's time to reassess your gut health and take care of your well-being from the inside out. Start by taking action today with the inclusion of fiber-rich whole foods, drinking plenty of water, minimizing sugar intake, and incorporating probiotics into your diet. Waiting until it's too late is not an option. Your digestive system is the foundation of life so why not invest in your future by taking good care of it?

By putting our own needs first and practicing self-love and self-care, we can overcome society's expectations and achieve true gratification in life. When we operate from a place of contentment, we experience a sense of peacefulness.

As a direct result, we become more confident, resilient, and better equipped to handle life's challenges. We are able to give back fully to our loved ones and communities, because we took the time to fill our own cup first.

We should all liberate ourselves from the societal norms that constrain us and prevent us from reaching our full potential. It is time to put ourselves first, without guilt or shame. The world needs empowered individuals who know their worth and can show up authentically in every aspect of their lives.

Today, let's take a step towards being at peace with ourselves - whether it be setting aside some alone time each day or saying no when we need rest, instead of overcommitting ourselves. Let's make self-love a priority so that we can live optimal lives full of joy, peace, and purpose!

Achieving inner peace is impossible without having the right people in your circle of influence. I can personally attest to the negative impact of being in a relationship where my partner constantly added more challenges to my already difficult life. The wrong people in your life can cause chaos and disruption, and therefore, it is crucial to choose your inner circle wisely. Your overall well-being depends on it, and you cannot afford to take this decision lightly.

Don't let toxic relationships hold back your potential for growth and success. That's why it's important to carefully choose who you allow into your life. You deserve to be surrounded by individuals who uplift and inspire you, not those who bring negativity and drama.

Think about the people in your current circle of influence. Are they helping or hindering your personal growth? Do they support and encourage you or do they constantly criticize and belittle you?

If someone is bringing more harm than good into your life, it may be time to cut ties with them. It can be difficult letting go of relationships that have been a part of our lives for a long time but sometimes it's necessary for our own well-being.

Surround yourself with positive influences - friends who believe in you even when things get tough; family members who offer unconditional Love; mentors or coaches that guide and motivate you toward success.

Remember: Your inner peace is worth protecting at all costs. Choose wisely when building your circle of influence because these are the people that will shape how far we go in life!

CHAPTER 5

FOCUSING ON YOUR SELF

There is power in leaving things where we find them. In life, we have a tendency to make excuses for others and to justify the reasons why they do what they do. It's time to stop making excuses for their behavior and start prioritizing your own well-being. Do not negotiate with yourself under any circumstances. You deserve to surround yourself with people who uplift you, support you, and treat you with respect. Don't settle for less than what you truly deserve.

Remember that negotiating with yourself only leads to self-doubt and a lack of confidence in your own decisions. Trust your instincts and know that walking away from toxic situations is the right choice.

So, stand firm in your beliefs, set boundaries when necessary, and don't let anyone make you feel guilty for putting yourself first. It's time to focus on your Self and leave things where they belong - behind you - as lessons learned on the path towards growth.

It is important for everyone to have a happy and prosperous life, free from negativity and toxicity. It is crucial to never let anyone discourage you or shake your confidence. You should always stay aware of your abilities and trust that everything will fall into place at the right time.

It's not easy to embrace new challenges and take risks, but they can be quite beneficial even if it means – and it often does - stepping out of your refuge. This is where personal growth thrives. Always keep an open mind and welcome new opportunities, knowing that failure is just a minor obstacle on the path to success. Quite frequently, it is that seeming failure that opens the path for greatness.

It's absolutely essential that you proactively seek out and surround yourself with positive influences that will inspire and uplift you, rather than letting negative influences bring you down. Moreover, as you prioritize your own well-being, it's crucial that you foster relationships built on mutual respect, honesty, and support.

You want to travel the path with like minds, but most importantly, don't allow yourself to be consumed by anyone else's agenda. Stay focused on your own goals and dreams, and surround yourself with people who will help you achieve them.

As the leader of your own journey, your success depends on the choices you make. Choose to avoid toxic relationships. Choose to surround yourself with positive and supportive people who encourage and motivate you toward your goals. Negative relationships can drain your energy and distract you from your focus.

And you need to understand 'relationships' in their broadest sense. This could be a partner, colleague, friend or relative. It is essential to keep your distance from people who bring you down and sap your last energy. Invest in relationships that uplift you and contribute to the best version of yourself.

Remember, your success depends on the people you surround yourself with, so choose wisely. It's always beneficial to be around individuals who share similar values and goals as you, and radiate positivity. This will not only bring joy into your life but also increase your chances of success.

Take charge of your life today! Seek out those who inspire

and support you, build relationships based on mutual respect and encouragement, and stay focused on achieving your dreams despite any challenges that may arise. With unwavering determination and a positive attitude, you can live a satisfying life, filled with happiness and success!

Learn to accept that we live in an imperfect world, and when people show us who they are, we must trust that this is who they really are.

Focusing on yourself is so important in life. Understanding your own needs and wants before entering into any discussion to assist anyone else is crucial to your growth. Take the time to reflect on what is truly important to you and what you are willing to compromise on. When dealing with others, it's important to recognize that everyone has their own motivations and interests so try to understand where they are coming from and what it will cost you.

Most importantly, don't take things personally or let emotions cloud your judgment. Stay focused on the end goal and remain steadfast. Remember that taking care of yourself and advocating for your own needs is not selfish, it's necessary for personal growth and success. By prioritizing self-care and self-advocacy, you'll be better equipped to handle challenging situations and navigate complex relationships with others.

One of the most important things you can do is to put yourself first and stay focused on your goals. You hold the power to make decisions that can positively impact your life. Right now, is the perfect time to take action and seize opportunities. Consider what you truly want out of life, whether it's financial stability, a prosperous career, meaningful relationships or all of the above.

Whatever your aspirations may be, they are attainable if you're willing to put in the effort and fully commit yourself. It's understandable to feel hesitant about stepping outside of your sanctum and taking risks. However, keep in mind that anything worth having requires effort and perseverance. Although the journey may have its challenges, with determination, success is inevitable.

Why would you wait any longer? - Start taking steps toward achieving your dreams today. Remember: You deserve everything this world has to offer. It's up to you whether or not you'll claim it as yours.

"You deserve everything this world has to offer. It's up to you whether or not you'll claim it as yours."

CHAPTER 6

INVESTING IN YOUR SELF

The process of investing in your Self is the best investment that you can ever make. The rewards are limitless and will last a lifetime. I will focus on four key elements to keep in front of your mind while making investments in your Self: Experience, Study, Master, and Healing.

Experience

It may seem strange to see experience as an investment. But everything you face in life – the good and the challenging - is the best teacher, and the wisdom you gain has the ability to strengthen your character. That's because once you experience something, it is hard to picture life before you encountered that experience. So let your experiences - especially in the things that you are most passionate about - be the guiding force for where you invest the most.

Remember, happiness is an inside job and can't be sustained by external forces. When you are truly living in your purpose and are passionate about living an intentional life, you will find eternal happiness. This is when you reap the rewards of investing in your Self, via authentic experiences.

Study

Equipping your Self with valuable knowledge will be the best investment you can make in your self-growth process. This means exploring your mind and world; it will require you to step out of your safe space and broaden your horizons. Maybe you cannot travel as often as you would like, but do not let that stop you from expanding your mind about life outside your own environment. Read a book, or watch a documentary about traditions, people, culture, and nature across the globe, and let your mind transport you there.

Reflecting on the impact of your choices after investing in life-changing experiences is crucial. Studying is the key to investing in yourself as it allows for continuous learning and growth, whether it's through formal education or self-study. Being equipped with more knowledge will empower you to handle with confidence any situation that may come your way.

Think of it as a review; it is imperative that we review the choices that we make in order to ensure we are in alignment with our authentic selves. We study things and people in order to better understand how we can utilize them to help us with our life's mission. We store all this knowledge to be used at various times in our lives. Once we have studied something long enough and become familiar with it, we are equipped for any test that comes our way.

This investment is not about gaining knowledge for bragging rights. This is about understanding yourself on the wider canvas of life and developing a wholesome appreciation for all things. As you expand your knowledge, stay true to yourself and don't let other opinions hold you back from achieving greatness and living a life without limits. Move towards the things that bring you great joy, and don't feel bad for doing so.

"It is imperative that we review the choices that we make in order to ensure we are in alignment with our authentic selves."

The important thing is when you are tested, that you are well enough to pass. Most people don't study for perfection, but for understanding things better. The more you prepare and study, the better equipped you are to deal with what life throws your way. This is why I believe in, "Staying Ready So You Don't Have To Get Ready." We need to approach our lives in the same manner.

One necessary aspect of studying, is that of Self. How many people can truly say that they study themselves more than anything else? We are so consumed with studying everything and everyone else, we often neglect to attend similar study to ourselves. Do you truly want to get better and be the best version of yourself? Well, the only way to get there is to invest in the time to study yourself.

Take notes of the things that you do on a daily basis. Are those things moving you closer to your purpose or moving you further? When you take the time to find these answers and address the things that are hindering you, that investment in studying will also reap great rewards.

Master

Mastering a skill or talent is another crucial aspect of investing in yourself. By becoming an expert at something, not only do you gain confidence, but you open up doors for new opportunities and potential income streams.

But that is only one level, and it is usually the one most of us focus on. Becoming, however, the master of your own Self, while it is a challenging process, once you achieve it, life transforms your challenges, and overtime it gets easier. When that happens, no one can manipulate or divert you from your purpose.

And best of all, you won't allow anyone to control you! It's a liberating feeling that you won't ever want to let go of. You deserve to have complete control over your own life and future. You possess the power to be great, but first, you must master yourself.

Consider all the successful people in history, they didn't reach their goals by chance or luck. They got there by being disciplined, focused, and determined. These are qualities that anyone can cultivate if they put their mind to it. So, don't settle for being average or let others dictate your life's path.

Take charge of your future and start mastering yourself today! I will say it again, it won't be easy, but nothing worth having ever is. However, believe me when I tell you that once you attain such a level of self-mastery, you will wonder how you managed to live any other way before. Your best Self awaits, and the time to take action and become the best version of yourself is now!

Healing

The one thing you don't want to do is to forget about healing yourself when investing in personal growth. Unfortunately, it happens to be the most overlooked element when investing in ourselves. Many people fail to realize that they need to heal. Some simply ignore the signs that their minds and bodies emit.

But let me tell you something – healing is essential to living a happy and fruitful life. Failing to heal from past traumas can be compared to internal bleeding. On the outside you may appear to be fine. But although the wounds may not be evident, they are causing significant harm to the person and can potentially jeopardize their well-being.

"Failing to heal from past traumas can be compared to internal bleeding"

Think about it for a moment. When was the last time you took some time out of your busy schedule to focus on yourself? To really listen to what your mind and body were telling you? If it's been a while (or never), then I urge you to start prioritizing self-healing.

Not only will this benefit your mental health, but it can also improve physical symptoms such as chronic pain or fatigue. By taking care of yourself first, everything else in life becomes easier – relationships with loved ones become stronger, work productivity increases and overall happiness levels rise.

Making investments in yourself is a pivotal step towards reaching your desired goals and living the life you've always envisioned. By gaining new experiences, you broaden your perspective and gain valuable insights that can aid you in making wise decisions. Taking the time to study and reflect on your experiences allows you to expand your knowledge and stay ahead of the curve.

Becoming a master of a skill requires dedication, hard work, and perseverance. However, the benefits are well worth it, as expertise sets you apart from others. Taking care of your Self through restorative practices like meditation or therapy is crucial to your physical and mental well-being. This enables you to pursue your true purpose without any obstacles.

Don't even think about waiting! Start investing in yourself today! Every small investment contributes to building a brighter future for yourself. Remember: we all possess the potential for greatness if we put our minds to it.

CHAPTER 7

PROTECTING YOUR SELF

The selfless must become Self first. It's a mental adjustment that needs to happen. In order to live a healthier life, it is crucial to put your Self before others. The problem is, if you are not mindful, takers have no boundaries and will take as much as they can. In fact, they will take everything you have until there isn't anything left. This is why you must be Self first. Set parameters and limits, and make sure you have enough for your Self before you give it to others.

There are many people in this world who will give you the shirt off their backs or their very last penny with no consideration as to how they will live. And while that seems noble, it is also careless. You can best take care of others when you learn how to take care of yourself, and a big part of that is knowing how much of yourself to give.

So, my response to this action is, don't. This is non-negotiable! Make sure you always account for your Self first before you give your time or resources away. And let us understand 'resources' on all levels — that which is tangible, but also your emotional and mental resources as well.

"I was that person who was always giving my energy, time, and resources. Until one day I was totally drained with nothing left for myself and the calvary never came to my rescue".

Don't wait for a similar thing to happen before you stand

guard. Learn from my mistakes and prioritize your Self, starting now. Don't wait until it's too late. The rewards will be worth it - improved mental health, increased productivity at work or school, and stronger relationships with loved ones. Imagine what could happen if everyone took care of themselves first. Let's lead by example.

As for me, it was through a process of self-restoration and self-actualization that I was able to reset, ground myself, and rebound to a place in time where I was no longer depleted. With a feeling of revitalization, I set aside new ground rules for how I spend my energies.

Keep in mind that we all start out with the same opportunity to put ourselves first. So don't feel guilty. See it as a necessity. Stop obsessing about what other people think. What you think, how you act and see your Self are what's important. This kind of unapologetic focus is how you protect your Self.

Make it a habit of meditating and resetting your mind each night before you sleep and focusing on the things you want when you first wake up. Think of your mind as something that needs to be reset for it to be at its optimum.

I spoke earlier of practicing mental 'house cleaning.' Each night, clear your mind of all the things that do not deserve to occupy that valuable real estate. Purge your mind of all the worthless 'tenants' that do not serve your best interest. Let go of the thoughts that are negative and anything that you have no control over.

Turn this into a routine and watch how efficient you become. You will now have the bandwidth to deal with the things that will move the needle forward in the direction of success. Once you have mastered the art of resetting your mind, move to the grounding phase.

Similar to electrical components, a poorly grounded system

will cause your appliances to be fried beyond repair. Likewise, the importance of finding an outlet, such as connecting with nature to ground your Self, is imperative.

Realizing our oneness with nature can make life easier and more satisfying. We are all interconnected through the universe and nature. Your inner Self holds the secrets of life, waiting for you to unlock them. Here is a simple practice. Connect with the earth by walking barefoot in the park, dipping your feet in the water at a nearby beach, or getting kissed by the sun.

"Realizing our oneness with nature can make life easier."

Rebounding as it pertains to the Self is an opportunity for a fresh start. The key to successfully rebounding is to realize that you have an opportunity to do things better. Releasing any emotional attachments to previous behaviors or feelings is crucial.

When we harbor past experiences and attach some sort of feelings and emotions to them, we have the hardest time moving forward. When we learn not to charge these feelings, and redirect those energies back to one's Self, is how you prevent being consumed with anyone else's issues.

By taking control of your emotions and redirecting them toward self-improvement, you can begin to see positive changes in all aspects of your life. Rebounding allows you to let go of negative experiences and focus on the present moment. It empowers you with a renewed sense of purpose and motivation that will drive you forward toward success.

Don't let past failures or setbacks hold you back any longer. Embrace the power of rebounding today and start living your best life! With dedication, perseverance, and a commitment to personal growth, anything is possible. So why wait? Take charge of your destiny now by embracing the transformative power of rebounding!

When you implement the process of reset, ground, and rebound, it becomes harder and harder for you to stray away from protecting your Self.

CHAPTER 8

I'M NOT SELFISH, I'M SELF FIRST

I'm not selfish. I'm self-first, and it's non-negotiable. That may sound harsh to some but hear me out.

Growing up, I was always taught to put others first. To be kind, considerate, and selfless. And while those are admirable qualities, when you don't understand and apply the balance; when you neglect to prioritize the security of your well-being, they can lead to burnout and resentment.

It wasn't until I hit rock bottom after a failed engagement, that I realized the importance of putting myself first. It just creeps up on you. I had been giving so much of myself to others that I had nothing left for myself. My mental health was suffering, my relationships were strained, and I felt lost.

That's when I made the decision - from now on, I will prioritize myself. And while I understood that the decision was best for me, it was easier said than done. It wasn't an easy choice to make. There were times when I felt guilty for saying no to a request; times when I felt selfish for taking time for myself.

But I kept pushing through, and over time, I began to see the benefits of prioritizing my own needs. My mental health improved, my relationships became healthier and more fulfilling, and I found a sense of purpose and direction in my life. Nowadays, when someone accuses me of being selfish, I simply smile and say, "I'm not selfish - I'm self-first."

And I truly believe that putting your Self first is not only necessary, but it's also the key to living a fulfilled life. You see, when you prioritize your own needs and desires, you become more confident in who you are and what you want out of life.

By taking care of your Self first, whether it be through self-care practices or pursuing your passions and goals without hesitation or apology, you set an example for others to do the same. And isn't that what we all ultimately want - to live our lives authentically and unapologetically?

So don't let anyone make you feel guilty for prioritizing your Self. It's time we start celebrating those who choose themselves over societal expectations or pleasing others. Because at the end of the day, being self-first means being true to ourselves - something that no one can ever take away from us. Making self-care a priority is crucial as it enables you to have the necessary energy and resources to provide effective care to others.

God forbid that we continuously place others over ourselves and ignore our own needs, it can lead to burnout and bitterness toward those we intend to assist. Thus, if you're feeling exhausted or weighed down by always putting others first, it's crucial to remember that taking care of yourself is necessary. You owe it to your Self.

It's important to remember that taking care of your Self should be a top priority. This is not a selfish act, but rather a necessity for your overall well-being and success. After all, if you don't prioritize your Self, who will? As they say, 'you can't pour from an empty cup.'

Think about it this way - when you reorganize the order of selfcare, you become more productive, focused, and energized. You'll be able to show up as your best Self in all areas of life including work, relationships or personal projects.

It's essential that we take care of ourselves before attempting to take on the world around us. Remember that by doing so, everyone benefits - including those closest to us who rely on our support and love every day.

> *"It's essential that we take care of ourselves before attempting to take on the world around us."*

However, there is a fine line between being Self-first and being selfish. And that line lies in empathy and consideration for others.

When you put your Self first, it doesn't mean disregarding everyone else's needs or feelings. It means finding ways to meet your own needs while also considering how your actions may affect those around you. For example, if you're feeling overwhelmed with work and need to take some time off to recharge, that's perfectly ok!

But instead of just taking off without any notice or communication with your team members or boss (which would be selfish), communicate openly about what you need, so that arrangements can be made accordingly (which is Self-first).

In short: Prioritizing yourself isn't inherently bad - but doing so at the expense of others' well-being definitely is. So, make sure to find balance by practicing empathy towards those around you, while still making sure your SELF comes first!

Remember to place a high level of importance on your well-being by setting boundaries with work or social obligations as needed. Take breaks throughout the day to recharge and indulge in activities that bring you joy. This will not only benefit you but also those around you. Make a promise to your Self today and stick to it!

So, if anyone ever makes you feel guilty for putting your Self first, remember this: Self-care isn't selfish; it's necessary! It's time we stop glorifying burnout culture and start valuing our mental health and well-being just as much as we value productivity.

CHAPTER 9

PUTTING YOUR SELF FIRST

It's easy to get caught up in the demands of everyday life and forget about our own needs. It is absolutely crucial that you tend to your own welfare and contentment by putting your Self first. Let me remind you, this is not selfish, but rather a fundamental requirement. Start by thinking of your "Self" as the inner God within and understand the importance of prioritizing your own needs. Embrace the fact that you are worthy of love, care, and attention just as much as anyone else.

When you take care of your Self first and appreciate your worth, you become more equipped to take on the challenges that life throws your way. You'll have more energy and mental clarity to tackle tasks with ease and confidence. Now you will be in a better position to choose those you want in your space.

Now there is mental and emotional strength to set clear boundaries in your relationships so that you're not constantly giving without receiving anything in return. This is not to suggest that you give to receive. But you need to stay aware of being taken advantage of.

This is a big part of protecting your Self. Love your Self enough to walk away from those unhealthy relationships. And pamper yourself every once in a while, without feeling guilty. Whether it's buying something nice or indulging in a favorite hobby, it should be all about you.

Taking time for your Self will look different for everyone, and that's ok. Take a relaxing bath or get a massage or pedicure. Whatever it is, just do you! And every time, take note as you get recharged to show up fully for others in your life. Keep trusting the power of your inner God and let it guide you toward a more balanced and fulfilling life.

You deserve to be happy, healthy, and fulfilled in all aspects of your life. By taking care of your Self first, you'll have more energy and resources to give back to those around you. There is no shame or guilt in focusing on your Self. You are not selfish. You are worthy and deserve the best out of life. When you focus on your well-being; when you prioritize your needs, everyone benefits - including the people closest to you. When you take care of yourself, you show the people you love that you care about them because now they will receive and benefit from the best version of you.

So, take a moment today and ask yourself: what do I need right now? What can I do to protect myself? Maybe it's some alone time or a night out with friends. Perhaps it's starting a new course or project that brings joy into your life. What you choose is not the issue. Choosing to do it and knowing you are doing it for yourself are the important and necessary factors.

Whatever it is, don't hesitate - go after it! Make sure that every day includes something just for YOU, because when we take care of ourselves first, everything else falls into place effortlessly! Remember: self-care isn't an option; it's essential!

Developing a habit requires consistent practice and the same applies to prioritizing your Self. You need to make it habitual. This book refers to the Inner God within you as the Self, which, when acknowledged, enables you to love, defend, respect, uplift, understand, and speak positively about yourself. Always remember to put your Self first.

By doing so, you can achieve a richer and more fulfilling life and master the art of manifestation. Combining the principles of Living in the Know and Living in the Now will help you manifest all that you desire in life.

> *"Combining the principles of Living in the Know and Living in the Now will help you manifest all that you desire in life".*

It's time to take control of your life and start living the life you deserve. Don't let negative thoughts or external factors hold you back from achieving greatness. You have the power within your Self to create a positive change in your life but it all starts with loving and respecting yourself.

Remember that self-care and self-love are vital ingredients for maintaining good mental and physical health. Contrary to popular belief, it is not a selfish act. Rather, it is a way to promote personal growth and emotional stability. When we love ourselves unconditionally, we radiate positivity that attracts abundance into our lives.

Take care of your physical health by exercising regularly and eating nutritious food. Nurture your mental health by taking breaks when needed, journaling about your feelings or seeking therapy if necessary. Keep in mind that every small step towards self-improvement counts towards creating a better version of yourself each day! So go ahead – put YOUR SELF FIRST – because YOU ARE WORTH IT!

CHAPTER 10

TRUST YOUR SELF

You know your own intentions, capabilities, and limitations better than anyone else. And the more you prioritize getting to know your Self, you will grow more confident in the decisions you make. Learn to rely on your own judgment. Don't second guess yourself just because someone has put that doubt in your mind. You won't always be right, but it is your mistake to learn from and to grow.

They say trust is to rely on another person because you feel safe with them and have confidence that they will not hurt or violate you. Let me suggest that before you extend blind trust, put the onus on 'knowing', first. Get to know others and learn to trust your judgement in that knowledge. That way, we can all be more forgiving of ourselves in the event that we are hurt or violated. Exposing ourselves to a level of unnecessary vulnerability is not healthy. So, it is important to know what a person can do, in the same manner as you know what you are capable of doing. This is where 'Being in the Know' again comes into play. Know that you have done your due diligence, rather than trusting that it is what it appears to be. Trust that you have done all in your power to be at ease with what you are faced with. This is how you put trust in your hands, rather than someone else's. This is how you safeguard yourself from unwarranted anxiety or disappointment.

I am sure you have had your share of experience in trusting others over yourself. Think about all the times when you trusted someone else and they let you down. It could have been a friend who betrayed your confidence, a colleague who took credit for your work or even a partner who cheated on you. These experiences can leave us feeling hurt, angry, and vulnerable.

I encourage you to take all that experience as your steppingstone toward trusting yourself. With that trust in Self, you have the power to prevent these negative outcomes. You can make choices that align with your values and goals, without worrying about someone else's agenda getting in the way.

Trusting your Self also means taking responsibility for your own actions and decisions, which is a key component of personal growth and development.

Of course, this doesn't mean that we should never seek advice or support from others. It's important to surround ourselves with people who uplift us and offer constructive feedback when needed. However, ultimately, it's up to us to decide which path we want to take in life. So, if you're feeling unsure or hesitant about something right now - whether it's a career move, relationship decision or any other major choice - I encourage you to listen closely to your instincts. Trust your Self enough to know that whatever happens next will be within your control.

Trusting your Self means having faith in your abilities to handle whatever life throws at you. It means being confident in making choices that align with your values and goals. And most importantly, it means not compromising on what matters most to YOU!

So next time someone tells you that trust is essential for building relationships – consider this: Trusting your Self first is building a relationship! Getting to know YOU, is building a relationship! Because when all else fails, YOU are the one person who will never let yourself down!

When you trust your Self, you gain confidence and self-assurance. You become more resilient in the face of challenges because you know that your decisions are based on what's best for YOU. It's very easy to get caught up in other people's opinions or societal expectations, but when you listen to your own inner voice, everything falls into place.

So, take a deep breath and trust your Self. Rest assured that every experience and lesson you've undergone has prepared you for this exact moment. I believe that whatever decision or path chosen ultimately leads towards growth and fulfillment.

"Rest assured that every experience and lesson you've undergone has prepared you for this exact moment".

Remember: Nobody knows YOU better than YOU do! So go ahead – make those tough choices with conviction, knowing that trusting your Self will lead to a happier life full of purposeful decisions made by none other than YOURSELF!

By doing so, you'll eliminate a lot of unnecessary stress and anxiety that comes with second-guessing yourself or seeking validation from others.

Trusting your Self is crucial to reaching your aspirations and leading a satisfying life. Trusting your abilities fosters self-assurance, making you more willing to take risks that can yield great rewards.

It's time to stop questioning your capabilities and hesitating. Those moments of doubt will not bring you any favorable outcomes. Instead, embrace your strengths and take ownership of your choices and actions. Be kind and gentle with yourself, and acknowledge that perfection is unattainable, but progress is.

Make a commitment right now to know who YOU are, even with your imperfections! Believe in the distinctive talents and gifts only YOU possess, setting you apart from everyone else!

I find that trusting your Self is like planting seeds of confidence. With time and nurturing, you can watch them grow into beautiful flowers. So, trust your Self and witness your aspirations manifest into reality.

CHAPTER 11

KNOWING YOUR TRUE SELF

In order to fully understand oneself, it is necessary to challenge the mind and embrace personal growth. As individuals, we are constantly evolving, and it's important to stay aware of our present state and how it relates to our ultimate purpose. By staying authentic and self-aware, we can better understand our destiny and who we are meant to become.

But how can we achieve this level of self-awareness and personal growth? It starts with a willingness to step outside our safe haven and push ourselves beyond what we thought was possible. This may mean trying new things, taking risks, or even facing our fears head-on.

It's also important to surround ourselves with positive influences that support our journey toward self-discovery. This could be through seeking out mentors or joining communities of like-minded individuals who share similar goals. Keep in mind that your mentors can also come from the pages of a book. Be inspired by those who have documented the journey to enlightenment and stay present to your own transformation.

Ultimately, the key to unlocking your full potential lies within you. By committing yourself to personal growth and embracing challenges as opportunities for learning and development, you can tap into your true purpose in life and become the best version of yourself.

So, stop procrastinating - take action today towards becoming more self-aware, pushing past limitations, and achieving your ultimate destiny!

Understanding your true Self is the key to loving yourself, wholly. Throughout this journey, we have emphasized the importance of living in the present moment. Simply believing in something is not enough. It is only when you unconditionally know the truth that you can avoid being misled or deceived.

Hope can be an illusion that keeps us in a state of delusion. When we hope without truly believing and trusting ourselves, manipulative people often use it to get what they want from us. But you can avoid falling for their tactics when you stay grounded in what you know to be true and apply critical thinking to every situation. By living in the "Now," you can avoid getting lost in fantasies and stay focused on the present moment.

Many people believe that their best life is yet to come but by mastering the art of living in the present, you can manifest anything you desire. Heaven is not some distant place that you reach after death; it is right here and now.

You have the power to create your own destiny, and it starts with taking control of your thoughts. Don't let others dictate what you believe or how you live your life. Instead, trust in yourself and follow your intuition.

Living life to the fullest demands you to be present in the now. Dwelling on future anxieties or past regrets will only deprive you of immediate joy and gratification. By living intentionally and mindfully, we can manifest our dreams into reality. Whether it's a fulfilling career, loving relationships or financial abundance - anything is possible when we focus our energy on positive outcomes.

So, take charge of your life today by embracing the power within you! You can achieve greatness beyond measure, if only you believe in your Self enough to make it happen. To truly live your best life and accomplish your goals, it's essential to maintain focus on the now.

Dwelling on the past or worrying about what's to come won't bring genuine happiness and success. By staying confident and present, you can transform your aspirations into reality. Stay in the present, and you'll be empowered to achieve your dreams.

This process involves being aware of your thoughts, feelings and actions toward your goals. In other words, you need to actively participate in the Now, to realize the outcome. Whether it's a career goal, a personal relationship, or a lifestyle change, remember, you must live in the "know"; you must have clarity about what you want and take steps towards making it happen. Don't wait for the afterlife to start living your best life - start now by embracing the power of the present moment.

Going forward, let this be your mantra: I will live in the KNOW, and stay informed about what is happening around me, and within me. I will live in the NOW and fully embrace the present moment.

Remember, these two ingredients are essential for molding and shaping our minds to survive in a world that often prioritizes external validation over internal fulfillment. By putting our needs first and cultivating a deep sense of self-love, we can rise above the shame that society tries to impose on us and create a life that is truly fulfilling.

It's time to elevate your life and embrace the abundance that you deserve. The power to create your own reality lies within, and it all starts with connecting with your true Self.

Think about it - how many times have you felt like something was missing in your life? How often do you find yourself wishing for more money, better relationships or greater success? The truth is these things are not outside of us; they are already within us waiting to be unlocked.

By embracing your Inner God, you can access an infinite

source of power to manifest your desires. You become an unstoppable force that attracts abundance effortlessly because you know your worth and believe in your Self.

"By embracing your Inner God, you can access an infinite source of power to manifest your desires."

So why wait? Start now, don't wait any longer to discover your true Self. Start with mindfulness meditation or journaling to connect with your innermost thoughts and feelings. Seek out mentors who can guide you on your journey toward enlightenment.

Always remember the oneness of your true Self, with God and as God. And that makes anything possible. This simple change will give you the key to unlocking your greatness. Keep reminding your Self that it's not selfish to prioritize your own needs, it's essential.

Say to your Self with confidence: "I'm not Selfish, I'm Self first, and It's Non-Negotiable."

About the Author

Mark Parris was born in Reading, England to Caribbean parents. After leaving the UK, Mark spent time in South America, and Canada, and eventually went to East Flatbush Brooklyn, NY. It was growing up in Brooklyn that helped to mold Mark's quick thinking and survival skills. He was drawn to philosophy and spirituality at a very early age.

Mark's strong sense of spirituality has helped him overcome numerous challenges faced in his life. He has decided to pass on some interesting advice to help others on their spiritual journey. In the event that you're looking to find inner peace, improve your mental well-being, and live a more fulfilling life, then Mark's advice is exactly what you need. His unique perspective on spirituality has helped countless individuals overcome their struggles and achieve true happiness.

Mark firmly believes that we all have the power within us to transform our lives for the better. By tapping into our spiritual selves and embracing positivity, we can unlock an endless supply of potential that will help us thrive in every aspect of life.

Do not waste any more time. Take control of your future and live the life you deserve. Mark's wisdom is the key to your enlightenment. His unwavering commitment to helping others attain spiritual growth makes him the perfect guide to success. Allow him to lead you towards a more fulfilling life.